Schaum

Best of Chopin

For Piano Solo

The primary object of this series is to serve as an introduction to the music of world-famous composers. These arrangements enable a student of modest profciency to gain an acquaintance with many master themes. Familiar music has been selected for maximum student appeal.

The choice of music in the collection is determined by its effectiveness for teaching purposes – based on over forty years' experience with thousands of piano students at the Schaum Music School in Wisconsin.

Additional composers in this series include:

Bach • Beethoven • Mozart • Schubert • Strauss • Tchaikowsky

EXCLUSIVELY DISTRIBUTED BY

HAL•LEONARD®
CORPORATION
7777 W. BLUEMOUND RD. P.O. BOX 13819 MILWAUKEE, WI 53213

Schaum Publications, Inc. • 10235 N. Port Washington Rd. • Mequon, WI 53092

Biographical Sketch

Frederic Chopin (SHOW-pan) is the greatest composer of music for the piano. All that had been said before him by the masters, Bach, Mozart or Beethoven, seems, after listening to Chopin, as if written in a language foreign to the instrument. When he speaks, it is the speech of one for whom this combination of wood, wire, iron and ivory is a human harp – a harp from which th most exquisite poetry is plucked. This Polish composer is rightfully named the poet of the keyboard.

Chopin was born in a small village near Warsaw, Poland, March 1, 1809. He died in Paris, October 17, 1849. In those brief forty years, he lived an existence devoted to art, a life that literally burned away his frail frame. He never married; he never gathered riches; and the honors heaped upon his as a virtuoso, the fame that greeted his wherever he went, brought his no message of joy. He was a dreamer of dreams.

Yet it must not be imagined that he was a sentimental dawdler. He labored over his compositions, working for hours, days, weeks, and months at one piece. He gave many lessons, but saved no money. A few visits to England, a trip to the island of Majorca in the Mediterranean Sea with the Sand family, where he nearly perished of lung trouble – this about comprises the history of Chopin. His life is written mainly in his music. To it we must go to understand the man.

Index

Les Sylphides Mazurka

F. CHOPIN, Op. 33, No. 2
Arr. by John W. Schaum

Note: Les Sylphides (lay sill-FEEDS) is the title of a famous ballet based on Chopin's music.

Waltz in E Minor

F. CHOPIN *
Arr. by John W. Schaum

*This waltz has no opus number because it was published posthumously (after the death of the composer).

Etude in E Major

F. CHOPIN Op. 10, No. 3
Arr. by John W. Schaum

Mazurka in B♭ Major

F. CHOPIN, Op. 7, No. 1
Arr. by John W. Schaum

Raindrop Prelude

F. CHOPIN, Op. 28, No. 15
Arr. by John W. Schaum

Nocturne in E♭ Major

F. CHOPIN, Op. 9, No. 2
Arr. by John W. Schaum

Andante cantabile

Butterfly Etude

F. CHOPIN, Op. 25, No. 9
Arr. by John W. Schaum

Prelude in A Major

F. CHOPIN, Op. 28, No. 7
Arr. by John W. Schaum

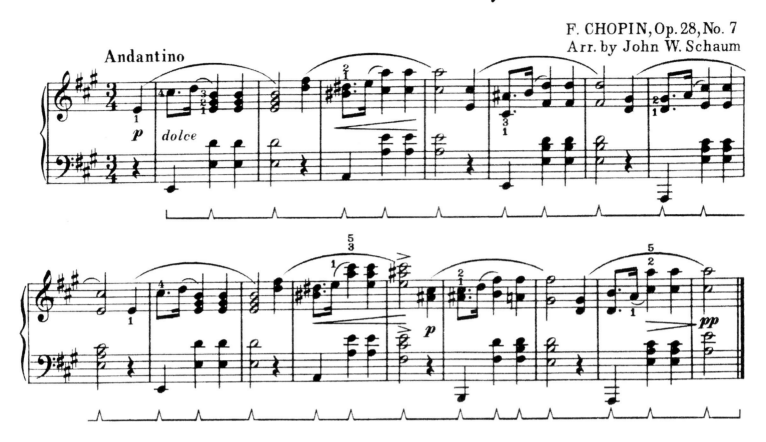

Prelude in C Minor

F. CHOPIN, Op. 28, No.20
Arr. by John W. Schaum

Prelude in B Minor

F. CHOPIN, Op. 28, No. 6
Arr. by John W. Schaum

Polonaise Militaire

F. CHOPIN, Op. 40, No. 1
Arr. by John W. Schaum

Fantasie Impromptu

F. CHOPIN, Op. 66
Arr. by John W. Schaum

Minute Waltz

F. CHOPIN, Op. 64, No. 1
Arr. by John W. Schaum

Grand Polonaise

F. CHOPIN, Op. 53
Arr. by John W. Schaum